TESTIMONIALS

"Through evolution, the human race is perpetually redefining itself. It does so by systematically pushing current boundaries because the human mind will not be confined to any limits.

Ian is the living embodiment of that statement.

Having him share his life's story with our audience was a truly vivifying experience, a now ever-echoing reminder of what truly matters during one's existence."

Vlad Gozman
Curator TEDxVienna
www.TEDxVienna.at

"When Ian first contacted me about riding a motorcycle on the "Wall of Death" I had built in a field, my first thought was "He's all talk!" But after meeting him I realised Ian is the type of person who turns his dreams to reality.

We all talk about what we would like to do but this book can help you develop that same determination Ian has to succeed. As I always say, "Be a shepherd, not a sheep.""

Colin Furze
Garage Inventor, Videographer, TV Host
www.ColinFurze.com

"I met Ian a few years back on his journey around the globe working toward his 100 goals. After reading this book, I not only learned how to go about achieving my goals, but more importantly I saw the proof in Ian's own life and hard work that by using his strategies it is possible to achieve your own goals. Ian definitely walked his talk!"

Clay Egan
Author, Speaker, Pro Rockcrawler
www.ClayEganRacing.com

"WOW. I love this book!!! When the inspirational speaker/author is inspired by another speaker/author's work, you know it is good stuff! I was honored to be asked to read a pre-publication copy of this book. What I didn't realize was how much of a WOW impact it would leave on me.

As a speaker and writer myself, I needed Ian and Vanessa's wise and encouraging words right now in my own life as I tackle yet more "out of the box" big new goals. Their book gave me an abundance of needed insights and actionable steps. It also sprinkled into my journey really great reminders of how and why to press on with my own overwhelming goals.

Don't let the easy breezy quick read fool you. This little book is packed with gems on every single page. Ian and Vanessa, thank you for putting together in one small book all the practical and inspirational words I need to go forward with my own big audacious goals!"

Kris Harty, shortCHICK with the Walking Stick
Speaker, Author, Show Host
"Stick to It – Step by Step!"
www.shortCHICK.com

7 Simple Steps to Goal Achieving Success

including 100 tips to help you achieve your goals and live the life you've always imagined

by

Ian Usher & Vanessa Anderson

Copyright

Copyright ©2014
by Ian Usher & Vanessa Anderson
Published by Wider Vision Publishing
All rights reserved

To find out how to publish
your own books take a look at
www.StudentScribbler.com

7 Simple Steps to Goal Achieving Success

ISBN 10:
0-9808653-3-6

ISBN 13:
978-0-9808653-3-2

CONTENTS

Introduction
How to use this book
7 Simple Steps to Goal Achieving Success
Step 1 – Write it down
Step 2 – Set a deadline
Step 3 – Work on your mindset
Step 4 – Develop your skillset
Step 5 – Take the first step
Step 6 – Continue to completion
Step 7 – Reward yourself
Further inspiration
Conclusion
About the authors
Suggested further reading
Also by the same author

INTRODUCTION

This is not a book about setting goals.

This is book about achieving goals so that you can create the lifestyle you have often imagined.

Achieving a goal is very different to setting a goal.

Many books have been written about goal setting. Setting a goal is easy. You simply think about something you would like to achieve in the future and write it down on a piece of paper. Your goal is set!

Achievement of that goal involves a bit more effort and determination.

If it were really as easy as writing your goals on a piece of paper we would all be ticking off items from our bucket list each and every day.

We all have different goals – some are simple, some are more challenging – but the process involved in beginning, working toward and ultimately completing most goals is the same.

This book has been written to help, inspire and focus you so that you can achieve your goals, whatever they may be, and so enjoy the life you have often imagined for yourself.

USING THIS BOOK

There are three separate aspects to the content of this book.

1) Tips

Firstly, there are 100 ideas and suggestions to help focus you to set your goals and work toward their successful completion.

These tips are divided into sections covering subjects such as mindset, skillset, getting started, overcoming challenges and more.

Not every tip will be relevant to every goal, every time. The book will be different each time you read it, depending which of your goals you are focused on.

2) Quotes

Along with each of the 100 tips there is a relevant and inspirational quote from one of the many great thinkers on motivation, inspiration and goal achievement.

Again, different quotes may "speak" to you at different times. Re-visit the book often for a regular top-up of inspiration.

3) Ideas and inspirations

Finally, on each page you will find a section for your own notes, entitled "My ideas and inspirations".

Always read this book with a pen or pencil in hand and jot down whatever comes to mind in the moment.

Re-read this book often. It will inspire you in different ways at different times as you progress through your goal achieving adventures.

Good luck on your journey.

Let's get started.

7 SIMPLE STEPS TO GOAL ACHIEVING SUCCESS

We were so tempted to call this section "7 Simple Steps to Goal Setting Success". It has such a lovely ring to it.

But this book is not just about "goal setting". It is about achieving your goals.

We all know that "goal setting" is very important, but please remember that setting your goal is only one of the steps on the journey to actually achieving your goal. You don't just want to set goals, do you? You want to achieve your goals.

Unfortunately the phrase "goal achieving" doesn't trip off the tongue with the same familiar ring that "goal setting" does. All too often when people talk about setting goals they are actually talking about how to accomplish or achieve their goal.

There is a simple and easy-to-follow process which can propel you toward the success you are striving for. The seven steps are outlined in the section below. There is a short introduction to each section, and a wealth of helpful tips.

For a free downloadable infographic on our:

"7 Simple Steps to Goal Achieving Success"

please visit our website at:

www.IanUsher.com

STEP 1
WRITE IT DOWN

Get your goal out of your imagination and on to a piece of paper. This then becomes a statement of intent.

The process of writing down your goal forces the subconscious to accept the commitment you have made to work toward your target.

1.1 Write down your goal

The first step toward achieving a goal is to write it down. Get it out of your head and onto paper.

This makes your goal a statement of intent and therefore much more concrete and real than an intangible thought.

99% of people don't take this vital first step and are therefore destined never to achieve their goals with any significance.

> The discipline of writing something down is the first step toward making it happen.
>
> Lee Iacocca

My ideas and inspirations

_____

_____

_____

_____

1.2 Make a list

If you have more than one goal that you would like to achieve, make a list. The power of writing down ALL of your goals cannot be over-emphasized.

Even if some of your goals are longer term, writing them down serves as a permanent reminder of what you want to achieve throughout your life.

Constant re-examination and visualization of the goal on your list will help to create the right mindset for achieving your objectives.

> *If you change your mindset you can change your actions. If you change your actions you can change your limits. If you change your limits you can achieve your goals.*
>
> Ian Usher

My ideas and inspirations

_____

_____

_____

_____

_____

1.3 Get SMART about your goal

SMART goals are:
- Specific
- Measurable
- Achievable
- Relevant
- Time-bound

See our website for a more in-depth discussion of SMART goals:

www.IanUsher.com/goals

> By setting a high-quality SMART goal you will enable yourself to be conscious, and your actions will carry more meaning. It is the execution of the SMART goals strategy that separates achievers from the rest of the people.
>
> Anna Stevens

My ideas and inspirations

_____

_____

_____

_____

_____

1.4 Write down your goal every day

As previously stated, the first step toward achieving a goal is to write it down. But if you really want to propel yourself toward your target as quickly as possible, write your goal down and reaffirm it on a regular basis.

Writing your goal down first thing each morning focuses your mind and ensures that you will make regular productive progress towards your ultimate success.

> It's the repetition of affirmations that leads to belief. And once that belief becomes a deep conviction, things begin to happen.
>
> Muhammad Ali

My ideas and inspirations

_____

_____

_____

_____

_____

STEP 2

SET A DEADLINE

Set a target date by which you will complete your goal. If your goal is a larger, more complicated challenge, break it down into smaller steps and determine a deadline for each separate step.

Put these important dates into your diary or computerized planner.

2.1 Make a plan

It may sound obvious, but the act of simply writing down your goal is only the first step toward your ultimate success. Next you will need to plan the route ahead, especially if your goal is complex and involves many steps.

Without a structured, well thought out plan you will lack any real direction.

Take the time to create a workable plan and the process of making it happen will become clearer. A plan will also give you something against which to measure your progress.

> A goal without a plan is just a wish.
> Antoine de Saint-Exupery

My ideas and inspirations

_____

_____

_____

_____

_____

2.2 Set a deadline

Set a date by which you will complete your goal. Make this very specific. This serves to focus your mind by adding an element of pressure. If you need to take time off from work, then book that time now.

Make your timeline challenging. If you think you have all the time in the world you are unlikely to focus, and you will inevitably delay taking the necessary first steps. A tight timeline is a critical part of achieving your goals, as it will force you to move forward quickly and decisively.

> *Crystallize your goals. Make a plan for achieving them and set yourself a deadline. Then, with supreme confidence, determination and disregard for obstacles and other people's criticisms, carry out your plan.*
>
> Paul J. Meyer

My ideas and inspirations

_____

_____

_____

_____

2.3 Start with an easy goal

If you are new to setting goals, start with a relatively easy one.

Success breeds success. The completion of one goal is a springboard to the next more challenging goal.

Develop a habit of success early on and it will be easier to work toward bigger and better goals as your confidence grows.

However, don't fool yourself by setting your sights so low that you don't stretch yourself at all.

> You have to set goals that are almost out of reach. If you set a goal that is attainable without much work or thought, you are stuck with something below your true talent and potential.
>
> — Steve Garvey

My ideas and inspirations

_____

_____

_____

_____

_____

2.4 Break down a large goal into smaller steps

It is easy to become overwhelmed by a challenging goal and start to see it as just too big to be achievable.

With these larger, longer term goals, it can be very helpful to break down the task into smaller, more easily achievable steps, which can be focused on and completed separately.

Each completed small step drives you closer to the achievement of the bigger goal.

> The secret of getting ahead is getting started. The secret of getting started is breaking your complex overwhelming tasks into small manageable tasks, and then starting on the first one.
>
> Mark Twain

My ideas and inspirations

_____

_____

_____

_____

_____

2.5 Set up a website

Accountability to others can be a big motivator for many would-be goal achievers. If you make a statement of intent and reveal your plans in an open and public forum then you have made a commitment not only to yourself, but to others too.

Set up a website, blog or social media site such as Facebook to share your ideas and receive feedback. This accountability will make it much harder to make excuses, or to delay taking the necessary steps that will propel you toward your ultimate success.

> It is a paradoxical but profoundly true and important principle of life that the most likely way to reach a goal is to be aiming not at that goal itself but at some more ambitious goal beyond it.
>
> Arnold Toynbee

My ideas and inspirations

_____

_____

_____

_____

_____

2.6 Use a diary for planning

Start using a diary to plan action steps for all your goals, and especially for larger, longer term challenges. Use a paper diary or an online diary planner – whichever you are most comfortable with.

Set out a realistic and detailed plan for tackling your short-term, mid-term and long-term timelines. Remember to include your target completion date.

Review regularly. What do you need to complete today? What will you do this week or this month?

> *Our goals can only be reached through a vehicle of a plan, in which we must fervently believe, and upon which we must vigorously act. There is no other route to success.*
>
> Pablo Picasso

My ideas and inspirations

_____

_____

_____

_____

STEP 3
WORK ON YOUR MINDSET

You can begin to work on your mindset long before you tackle your first goal.

Develop a positive, "glass half-full" approach to every aspect of your life, including your thoughts about how you will achieve your goals.

Read inspirational books, hang out with other motivated people, and believe in your own abilities.

Work on your own attitude at every opportunity.

This should remain a lifelong process.

3.1 Adjust your attitude

You need to develop a habit of thinking positively. Your attitude is one of the key precursors for the successful completion of your goals.

If you are constantly complaining about all the challenges you face, or you keep telling yourself that you can't possibly achieve the task you have set, you are positioning yourself for failure.

Try hard to ensure that your attitude is positive at all times.

> If you don't program yourself, life will program you!
>
> Les Brown

My ideas and inspirations

_____

_____

_____

_____

_____

3.2 Get inspired by your goals

Develop a passion for your goals. They are on your list because they are things you want to achieve, or things that will make a big difference in your life. Convert any negative "can't do" thoughts into positive actions by finding out more about your goal.

Research online or look for videos on YouTube of others who have already achieved the same or similar goals. Become motivated by their passion and success. Use this excitement to become more and more inspired about what you want to achieve.

> Twenty years from now you will be more disappointed by the things that you didn't do than by the ones you did do. So throw off the bowlines. Sail away from the safe harbor. Catch the trade winds in your sails. Explore. Dream. Discover.
>
> Mark Twain

My ideas and inspirations

_____

_____

_____

_____

_____

3.3 Set your sights on the end result

Consider how it will be when you finally achieve your goal.

Spend some time imagining yourself in the future as if your goal has already been completed. Contemplate what it will feel like and how this might change your life.

The more you can see your goal as complete, the more your subconscious mind will believe it to be so. Your mind will then more automatically work toward achieving this outcome.

> The future you see is the future you get.
> Robert G Allen

My ideas and inspirations

_____

_____

_____

_____

_____

3.4 Use visualization

Many athletes and top performers use visualization techniques to aim for peak performance.

Picture the perfect result in your mind's eye. Visualize your best performance from your own viewpoint. Then see it as if you were watching your performance from another participant's viewpoint.

Also try visualizing a flawless performance as if seen from a camera viewpoint, edited to make the perfect film of your achievement.

> Imagination sets the goal picture which our automatic mechanism works on. We act, or fail to act, not because of will, as is so commonly believed, but because of imagination.
> Maxwell Maltz

My ideas and inspirations

_____

_____

_____

_____

_____

3.5 Dream big

Set big goals to achieve great things. Don't be afraid to set your sights high.

Big goals take you outside of your comfort zone and motivate you for success.

Big goals will help you identify both your strengths and your weaknesses.

Big goals inspire you and give you vision.

> Shoot for the moon. Even if you miss, you'll land among the stars.
>
> Les Brown

My ideas and inspirations

_____

_____

_____

_____

_____

3.6 Make your goals realistic

While dreaming big is very important, being realistic is also vital. Don't set yourself up for failure by making your goal so difficult that you cannot possibly believe in it.

For example, setting a goal to run a marathon within the next couple of months is great if you are already reasonably fit and healthy. However, if running is new for you, or if your fitness is below par, be more pragmatic.

Maybe set a different or less challenging short term goal, and adjust the timeline for your bigger, more ambitious goal.

> The world wasn't formed in a day, and neither were we. Set small goals and build upon them.
>
> Lee Haney

My ideas and inspirations

_____

_____

_____

_____

_____

3.7 Keep an open mind

Goals aren't always achieved in exactly the manner you might imagine. You need to be open to all sorts of possibilities and suggestions. Anticipate that the journey to your goal may change or be modified.

Learn to stay open to all possibilities. Learn never to say "no" until you have fully explored a suggestion. You never know from where an idea, inspiration or assistance may materialize along the way. This could help with the overall achievement of your goal in a way you had not imagined.

> Minds are like parachutes - they only function when open.
> Thomas Dewar

My ideas and inspirations

_____

_____

_____

_____

3.8 Develop a positive outlook

To achieve anything significant you need to be able to believe in yourself. You have to develop a "glass half-full" approach to everything in life. See the positives in all situations and be able to spot possibilities when they present themselves. Opportunities are not always obvious – they are often only visible to people who demonstrate a positive outlook on life.

Try catching yourself if you react negatively and see if you can see why you have this tendency. The more you become aware and conscious of any negativity in your responses, the easier it is to practice transforming them positively.

> Think like a queen. A queen is not afraid to fail. Failure is another stepping stone to greatness.
>
> Oprah Winfrey

My ideas and inspirations

_____

_____

_____

_____

_____

3.9 Listen to audio programs

There are some great audio programs available on CD or to download. Listen to inspirational presenters who offer positive messages. This will continually program your mind with positive thoughts and positive behavior patterns.

The internet and YouTube are great resources for finding downloads.

> Listen to many people, but talk to few.
> William Shakespeare

My ideas and inspirations

_____

_____

_____

_____

_____

3.10 Read positive books

Books represent another wonderful source of positive input. Read some of the personal development classics, such as Napoleon Hill's "Think and Grow Rich", or Steven Covey's "7 Habits of Highly Effective People".

Surround yourself with any number of these books and read and re-read. You will often take on a new and different perspective from an author depending on where you are on the road to the ultimate achievement of your goal.

See the "Suggested Further Reading" section at the end of this book, or visit www.IanUsher.com/goals for more suggestions and links.

> The man who doesn't read good books has no advantage over the man who can't read them.
>
> Mark Twain

My ideas and inspirations

_____

_____

_____

_____

3.11 Attend a seminar

Seminars are well worth considering for motivation and inspiration. Being around other positive, goal-oriented people is transferable. Networking may just give you the contacts you need to assist others with their goals and make progress toward your own.

However, the nature of many of these seminars is to draw on your enthusiasm, so take care to research your options thoroughly. Check on-line reviews and forums to ensure you select the best seminar for your particular goal.

Part with any money wisely that could otherwise be used to fund your final objective.

> High achievement always takes place in the framework of high expectation.
>
> Jack and Garry Kinder

My ideas and inspirations

_____

_____

_____

_____

3.12 Listen to powerful, uplifting music

Music has an incredibly powerful emotional impact. Make a playlist of music that inspires and uplifts you. Try to avoid lyrics that convey sadness, pain or negativity.

For you this may be classical music, or it may be spiritual. It might even be pumping rock music and inspiring anthems. It can be anything, as long as it makes you feel good, positive and motivated.

Use it as a regular background soundtrack to lift your mood and revive your enthusiasm to succeed.

> *If a man does not keep pace with his companions, perhaps it is because he hears a different drummer. Let him step to the music which he hears, however measured or far away.*
> Henry David Thoreau

My ideas and inspirations

_____

_____

_____

_____

3.13 Watch an inspirational movie

Movies are great for inspiration. They make us laugh and cry, but above all they stimulate passion and thought. They remind us that we are all in this together and this keeps our spirit strong and determined.

There is nothing more encouraging than watching the story of someone else who has achieved their goal, especially if success comes through adversity.

Here are just a few of the many inspirational films you can watch.

Moneyball, National Velvet, Rocky, A Wonderful Life, Phar Lap, The Bucket List, The Pursuit of Happyness, Billy Elliot, Braveheart, The Way, Schindler's List, Into the Wild….

> Vision is the art of seeing the invisible.
>
> Jonathan Swift

My ideas and inspirations

_____

_____

_____

_____

3.14 Your goal has already been achieved!

Unless you are breaking completely new ground, it is always encouraging to know that others just like you have already achieved your goal.

Find some examples of how, when and where your goal has been previously achieved. Take inspiration from these stories and note any relevant tips that might help you.

Know that if someone else can do it, there is no reason at all why you can't too.

> That some achieve great success is proof to all that others can achieve it as well.
>
> Abraham Lincoln

My ideas and inspirations

_____

_____

_____

_____

3.15 Spend time with other goal-oriented people

The circle of people that make up your peer group will have a huge influence on your outlook and attitude. Spend time with people who set their sights high and have already accomplished their goals, or who have similar goals and visions as you.

It is important to be around people who inspire you to find the best within yourself. Not only will they influence you, but you too will have an effect on them.

Avoid spending time with anyone that consistently negates your ambition or tells you your goal is unachievable. They will only hinder your progress.

> ... especially when the whole group is together, each bringing out all that is best, wisest, or funniest in all the others. Those are the golden sessions, when the whole world, and something beyond the world, opens itself to our minds as we talk.
>
> C.S. Lewis

My ideas and inspirations

_____

_____

_____

_____

3.16 Develop a hunger for your goal

It is easy to begin your journey with enthusiasm and excitement, but you must maintain a hunger to achieve your goal or it may never come to fruition.

Many people set New Year resolutions, but never go on to achieve their goals once the initial motivation has diminished. You must maintain your hunger by continually recommitting yourself to your goal and your vision.

Develop daily rituals that reconnect you to your purpose, reminding you that it is just a matter of time before your goal is achieved.

> *If you do not develop the hunger and courage to pursue your goal, you will lose your nerve and you will give up on your dream.*
>
> Les Brown

My ideas and inspirations

_____

_____

_____

_____

3.17 Increase your energy levels

To be a successful, goal-oriented person it is important to see all aspects of maintaining your mental and physical health as contributory factors to victory.

Give yourself a health check. Check your diet, your physical and mental wellbeing and your fitness levels. Improvements in any of these areas will help boost your energy levels and "feel good" factor. Avoid quick fixes and look for longer term, sustainable options to maximize your ongoing energy.

Monitor when during the day or evening you are at your most energized and try to use this time to work on your goal achievement activities.

> The higher your energy level, the more efficient your body. The more efficient your body, the better you feel and the more you will use your talent to produce outstanding results.
>
> Anthony Robbins

My ideas and inspirations

_____

_____

_____

3.18 Embrace change

You can't achieve your greatest goals by being the person you are now. You need to grow and expand your state of mind in order to achieve beyond the level at which you currently perform.

Do this by using as many of the ideas in this section as possible. Accept that you will need to continuously develop and learn new skills, habits and attitudes in order to achieve significant new things.

> Change is inevitable in life. No matter how much we would like things to stay the same, they won't. Embrace change when it happens, as there is usually nothing you can do about it. Change forces us out of our comfort zone, and requires us to re-assess our life. The outcome can often be startling.
>
> Ian Usher

My ideas and inspirations

_____

_____

_____

_____

_____

3.19 Expect to succeed

Attitude is of the utmost importance when setting and achieving goals.

Program your mind for success by expecting to succeed.

The more you believe in yourself and your actions, the easier it is to make the right choices that will ultimately guarantee your success.

Know that your goal IS achievable.

> I have learned that if one advances confidently in the direction of his dreams, and endeavors to live the life he has imagined, he will meet with a success unexpected in common hours.
>
> Henry David Thoreau

My ideas and inspirations

_____

_____

_____

_____

_____

3.20 Act as if your goal is already achieved

An important step toward creating the right mindset is to act as if you have already achieved your goal.

Once you start growing and becoming a person capable of achievement, you can start to expect success.

Talk and act as if the goal is already a done deal.

Before you know it, it will be.

> Dream it to be it.
>
> Walt Disney

My ideas and inspirations

_____

_____

_____

_____

_____

STEP 4
DEVELOP YOUR SKILLSET

It is quite possible that a new goal will necessitate learning a new skill or will require some form of personal growth.

Figure out what new knowledge you will need, or what new skills you will have to develop.

Find the best source for gaining this knowledge and invest wisely to develop the assets you need.

4.1 Research your goals

Many goals will require that you do some research. Don't assume that you know all the answers to achieving your goal.

Technologies progress all the time and there is a wealth of knowledge to be found both on the internet and in local community groups.

You will have a much better chance of achievement if you find out as much as possible about your goal. Research will also build your excitement and enthusiasm and propel you toward action and ultimately to success.

> Study strategy over the years and achieve the spirit of the warrior. Today is victory over yourself of yesterday. Tomorrow is your victory over lesser men.
>
> Miyamoto Musashi

My ideas and inspirations

_____

_____

_____

_____

_____

4.2 Develop your skillset

If achieving your goal involves skills that you do not yet possess, there is no alternative – you are going to have to learn and develop those skills.

The research you have undertaken will let you know what you need to learn.

Investigate local community classes. Learning a language, for instance, is often easier in a small group of people that all motivate and encourage each other. If your goal is adventure based, check out local clubs and be sure to visit for information and inspiration.

> Wisdom is knowing what to do next, skill is knowing how to do it, and virtue is doing it.
>
> David Starr Jordan

My ideas and inspirations

_____

_____

_____

_____

_____

4.3 Read an instructional book

Study what others have written about your chosen goal subject. Just one idea from a book could be the key that propels you toward the achievement you seek.

Manuals are often very expensive. If your subject is technical, visit your local library or check eBay and other such websites, where you may find second hand copies.

Remember, the more you learn about your subject, the more confident you will be as you approach your goal.

> We are the creative force of our life, and through our own decisions rather than our conditions, if we carefully learn to do certain things, we can accomplish those goals.
>
> Stephen Covey

My ideas and inspirations

_____

_____

_____

_____

_____

4.4 Book a course

Sometimes it may be necessary to invest in a course or training session to get practical hands-on instruction from experts in your goal subject.

By learning from others already skilled in what you are trying to achieve you can shorten your timeframe significantly.

You will learn a skillset much more quickly and most likely gather a lot of useful information at the same time.

Invest in yourself to accelerate your success.

> Learn of the skilful; he that teaches himself, has a fool for his master.
>
> Benjamin Franklin

My ideas and inspirations

_____

_____

_____

_____

_____

4.5 Apply focus

Staying focused can help you accomplish almost anything in life.

Make "to-do" lists for tasks related to your goal and check items off your list before moving on. This will help keep you focused on one task at a time.

Keeping a clean and organized work-space can help you focus and work on your goals with much more concentration.

Make time for breaks – take at least a 10 minute break for every hour of work. Do something completely different and then return to focus on your goal tasks, refreshed and with a clear mind.

> You don't have to be a fantastic hero to do certain things to compete. You can be just an ordinary chap, sufficiently motivated to reach challenging goals.
>
> Edmund Hillary

My ideas and inspirations

_____

_____

_____

_____

4.6 Ask for help

Share your goals and ideas with others in your peer group. They may be able to offer suggestions, or even assist you with your objectives.

You too may be able to help them toward their own goals.

However, be mindful of who you share your thoughts with. Ensure that you mix with positive and supportive people, and avoid the negative ones who may hold you back.

> It is one of the most beautiful compensations of life that no man can sincerely try to help another without helping himself.
>
> Ralph Waldo Emerson

My ideas and inspirations

_____

_____

_____

_____

4.7 Find a mentor

Find someone who has already achieved your goal and ask them to be your mentor. Such a connection will provide immense confidence and motivation.

If you are striving to achieve something new, or don't know anyone who has achieved the same or similar challenge, find a positive, motivational mentor who can still support and encourage you to suceed.

Remember that a mentor is much more than a teacher. A mentor should be able to genuinely identify where you need to grow and then assist in developing any necessary characteristics. A mentor should never want you to be just like them.

Choose wisely!

> A single conversation across the table with a wise person is worth a month's study of books.
>
> Chinese Proverb

My ideas and inspirations

_____

_____

_____

_____

STEP 5
TAKE THE FIRST STEP

It is important not to procrastinate. The moment when real action is required is often when many goals fall by the wayside.

You don't need to wait until everything is just right. Get started now and make adjustments as you go along. Take that first step. If you wait for the moment when everything is in perfect alignment you will never get started.

Try to make your first step an easy one to commit to. This will encourage you to make it as soon as possible, so you quickly begin the journey toward achieving your goal.

5.1 Take the first step

There is no time like the present to get started on your goal.

If you plan to wait until everything is in place before you start to tackle your goal, you may never get started.

Don't put off impending tasks to a later date or leave important actions to the last minute.

Take action now!!

> If we wait for the moment when everything, absolutely everything is ready, we shall never begin.
>
> Ivan Turgenev

My ideas and inspirations

_____

_____

_____

_____

_____

5.2 Do the important things first

It is far too easy to be busy doing things that are unimportant.

Get busy with the important stuff - the strategic tasks that will move you quickly toward the achievement of your goal.

Break your goal down into small sections and then pick the most important parts to address before you do anything else.

> The key is not to prioritize what's on your schedule, but to schedule your priorities.
>
> Stephen Covey

My ideas and inspirations

_____

_____

_____

_____

_____

5.3 Be accountable to someone else

If you haven't made yourself publicly accountable by declaring your intent on your website or blog, then find someone who you can be accountable to in person.

Let them know your end target and the steps you plan to follow on the path to your goal. Give them permission to hold you accountable.

Tell them to keep a regular check on you, and they can help you maintain a steady focus on your objectives.

> If we want unity, we must all be unifiers. If we want accountability, each of us must be accountable for all we do.
>
> Christine Gregoire

My ideas and inspirations

_____

_____

_____

_____

_____

5.4 Use your time productively

Get your priorities right. Find time to work regularly on your goals. Plan every day ahead so you are clear in advance about what you need to do.

Don't waste your time re-organizing your email inbox or re-arranging your sock drawer!

Try to be as efficient as possible when managing your time. Listen to motivational audios while driving your car. Work on your plan while traveling by train.

Time used well will accelerate you toward your end goal.

99 Discipline is the bridge between goals and accomplishment.
Jim Rohn

My ideas and inspirations

_____

_____

_____

_____

_____

5.5 Use visual reminders

Collect visual imagery or written reminders of your goals and place these in easily seen places around your home or in your workspace.

Put a photo of your goal by the mirror in the bathroom so you see it every morning. Write a reminder or use an inspirational quote that you can stick to the inside of the front door, so it is the last thing you see as you leave the house.

Put a Post-It note on the TV suggesting that you could be more productive with your time than watching the latest soap opera episode! Use as many locations as you can to put up motivational reminders to keep you enthused and on track.

> Visualize this thing that you want, see it, feel it, believe in it. Make your mental blue print, and begin to build.
>
> Robert Collier

My ideas and inspirations

_____

_____

_____

_____

5.6 Computer desktop background

Find an image that reminds you of your goal and use this as a permanent computer desktop background picture.

Do the same on your tablet or phone. Constant visual reminders of your goal will cement a mental picture in your mind and act as a cue for you to take whatever actions may be needed.

Remember to change these as you complete each of your goals.

> Think about your goals at every opportunity throughout the day.
>
> Brian Tracy

My ideas and inspirations

_____

_____

_____

_____

5.7 Screensaver images

It is possible on most computers to set your screensaver so that it will display pictures from your computer albums or online directories.

Take time to create a folder of inspirational images that reflect your current goals. Search online for images and quotations that you could also download.

Try joining our "goal quotes" community on Google+ for relevant images and quotations.

Again, constant visual reminders are great for programming your mind to concentrate more effectively on achieving your goal.

> What the mind can conceive and believe, it can achieve.
> Napoleon Hill

My ideas and inspirations

_____

_____

_____

_____

_____

5.8 Make a vision board

A "vision board" is another useful tool if you have many goals or your goal involves many aspects.

Sit quietly and review exactly what you want to achieve. Some images may come to mind to get you started. Collect pictures, quotes and other relevant items that symbolize the outcome you will achieve upon completion of your goals

Put this somewhere where you will see it often, and add to it regularly to keep motivation high. This will become an ongoing inspirational and visual cue for action.

> Fix your eyes on perfection and you make almost everything speed toward it.
>
> William Ellery Channing

My ideas and inspirations

_____

_____

_____

_____

_____

5.9 Document your progress

If you made yourself accountable to others on a blog or website then publish an on-going report of the actions you have taken, the results you have achieved and the progress you have made. Set a date for this purpose each month in your diary.

This accountability to others helps focus your commitment both to yourself and the goals you have set.

Remember to photograph different stages of the journey on the way to your goal. Add pictures to your updates to remind you of the success you have achieved so far. This will motivate you toward further achievement.

> Take the pains required to become what you want to become, or you might end up becoming something you would rather not be.
>
> Donald Trump

My ideas and inspirations

_____

_____

_____

_____

5.10 Apply positive internal dialogue

As you work toward your goal, be aware of your own inner and outer dialogues.

Be careful of the words you use in order to maintain a positive attitude.

Avoid words like "problem" or "setback", as they have negative connotations. If you are encountering difficulties, use a word like "challenge", which promotes a much more positive perspective.

Never say "I can't", "I'll try" or "that's impossible".

> Try not. Do. Or do not. There is no try.
>
> Yoda

My ideas and inspirations

_____

_____

_____

_____

5.11 Do it even when you don't want to

Some mornings you just don't feel like doing the things you know you should. If at these times you can force yourself to do the important things, progress toward your goal will be accelerated.

Fight against these feelings – it's only your mindset that needs adjusting. When you've completed those important tasks, reward yourself and reflect on how good you feel about your positive action.

Those who do what others cannot, or will not, are usually the ones who enjoy greater success.

> Dreaming is wonderful, goal setting is crucial, but action is supreme. To make something great happen you must get busy and make it happen. Take that action step today that will put you on your path to achievement.
>
> Greg Werner

My ideas and inspirations

_____

_____

_____

_____

5.12 Do what you need to do, not what you want to do

Reflect on whether your planned activity will propel you toward the completion of your goal. Or is it just a time-filler that will have little impact on what you are trying to achieve?

When your goal is achieved, that's the time to enjoy the fruits of your efforts, and to do the things you want to do.

Maintain focus on the end result you are striving for and keep working diligently in that direction.

> The victory of success is half won when one gains the habit of setting goals and achieving them. Even the most tedious chore will become endurable as you parade through each day convinced that every task, no matter how menial or boring, brings you closer to fulfilling your dreams.
>
> Og Mandino

My ideas and inspirations

_____

_____

_____

_____

STEP 6
CONTINUE TO COMPLETION

The path to the ultimate completion of your goal is unlikely to be a straight and simple one. Do not give up when you come up against the first or any subsequent obstacle.

Always keep the end result in focus. Maintain your levels of excitement and enthusiasm and keep moving forward.

See each difficulty you encounter as an opportunity for learning and growth.

6.1 Make a commitment to yourself

Promise yourself that no matter what obstacles you encounter you will continue toward your goal.

Make an absolute no-compromise commitment to yourself that you will complete your goal.

Write this down and pin or stick it somewhere at home and work where you can read and reconnect with your commitment on a daily basis.

> *Obstacles are those frightful things you see when you take your eyes off your goal.*
>
> Henry Ford

My ideas and inspirations

_____

_____

_____

_____

_____

6.2 Take action every day

No matter how small, try to achieve one thing each day that moves you toward your goal.

This daily commitment will build up exponentially over time. Do not halt this forward progress until your end result has been achieved.

If you do this in a consistent manner you will achieve your goal much quicker than you might have expected.

> Know what you want to do, hold the thought firmly, and do every day what should be done, and every sunset will see you that much nearer to your goal.
>
> Elbert Hubbard

My ideas and inspirations

_____

_____

_____

_____

_____

6.3 Reaffirm your goal every day

If you really want to focus and accelerate your progress, take a couple of minutes each morning to reaffirm your current goal. This can become a habit on waking up – a few minutes of quiet reflection to remind yourself of your progress, imminent tasks and to contemplate your future success.

This will help to focus you for the day and you are much more likely to take positive steps forward on a regular basis.

> How am I going to live today in order to create the tomorrow I am committed to?
>
> Anthony Robbins

My ideas and inspirations

_____

_____

_____

_____

_____

6.4 Enjoy the journey

Sometimes it is the journey on route to the destination that really counts.

It isn't always the achievement of the goal that is most important. It is often the overall adventure that provides the greatest experiences and insights.

Progressing toward your goals is what life is about. This is when you can learn more about yourself and others. Take the time to enjoy the journey along the way.

> For a long time it had seemed to me that life was about to begin..... But there was always some obstacle in the way, something to be gotten through first, some unfinished business, time still to be served, a debt to be paid. Then life would begin. At last it dawned on me that these obstacles were my life.
>
> Alfred Souza

My ideas and inspirations

_____

_____

_____

_____

6.5 Flexibility is the key

Plan for everything but also allow for the unexpected. There is little doubt that you will stumble upon unforeseen obstacles. Life will blindside you. Changes are inevitable. However, you will learn from all of these challenges, especially if you maintain a flexible outlook.

Drop any ideas of controlling the course of your goal. You cannot be too rigid in how you plan to do things. Accept that you may need to adapt your plans to suit changing circumstances.

Flexibility enables you to turn challenges into opportunities. Opportunities turn into unique experiences that result in goal achievement success.

> Life will blindside you. That is almost certain. How you respond is up to you.
>
> Ian Usher

My ideas and inspirations

_____

_____

_____

_____

6.6 Identify your negative traits

We all have some negative traits. If you can allow yourself to see these aspects of your character you will be able to practice positive transformation.

It is often in moments of stress or challenge that our negative personality traits are uncovered. Use these moments positively to develop self awareness, but remember to consider your positive attributes too.

Talk to your mentor. It is easy to deny your own negative characteristics but that can hamper your success.

> He who would be useful, strong, and happy must cease to be a passive receptacle for the negative, beggarly, and impure streams of thought; and as a wise householder commands his servants and invites his guests, so must he learn to command his desires and to say, with authority, what thoughts he shall admit into the mansion of his soul.
> James Allen

My ideas and inspirations

_____

_____

_____

_____

6.7 Don't go back to your old ways

Review regularly and write down all the positive changes you have made since starting your goal achievement journey.

Check to see if you have wavered in your commitment. Success often relies on you making challenging alterations to your lifestyle. It is often very easy to revert to the coziness of old habits.

Read again the tips and suggestions in this book. Identify where you may have slipped back into your previous routines. Sometimes you will be surprised where this may have occurred without you even noticing!

> Thoughts lead on to purposes; purposes go forth in action; actions form habits; habits decide character; and character fixes our destiny.
>
> Tyron Edwards

My ideas and inspirations

_____

_____

_____

_____

6.8 Don't run from problems

Problems, better referred to as challenges, when viewed in a positive light, promote creative thinking.

Don't blame circumstances or other people. Take ownership of your challenges and deal with them head-on.

It is often from tackling challenges that the greatest leaps forward are made.

> The best years of your life are the ones in which you decide your problems are your own. You do not blame them on your mother, the ecology, or the president. You realize that you control your own destiny.
>
> Albert Ellis

My ideas and inspirations

_____

_____

_____

_____

_____

6.9 Shed your excuses

Firstly be aware that all excuses will hamper your road to success. An excuse provides a reason not to deal with a challenge.

Sometimes our excuses are so good that we convince ourselves that a problem is real. But the problem does not go away.

Practice taking positive action when an excuse forms in your mind. A quick and spontaneous action will often dispel your justification for not dealing with an obstacle.

> *Don't say you don't have enough time. You have exactly the same number of hours per day that were given to Helen Keller, Pasteur, Michelangelo, Mother Teresa, Leonardo da Vinci, Thomas Jefferson, and Albert Einstein.*
>
> H. Jackson Brown

My ideas and inspirations

_____

_____

_____

_____

_____

6.10 Be prepared to make sacrifices

It is inevitable that the achievement of your goal will involve making some sacrifice to your lifestyle.

Whether it be time, money, commitment or personal relationships, be prepared to give up some aspect of, or make changes to, your current way of life to achieve your lifetime goals.

Remember that we only live this life once – you are on this journey to step outside mediocrity. Sacrifice may be an essential part of your voyage.

> He who would accomplish little must sacrifice little; he who would achieve much must sacrifice much; he who would attain highly must sacrifice greatly.
>
> James Allen

My ideas and inspirations

_____

_____

_____

_____

6.11 Don't worry about what others think

Only a small proportion of the population will achieve their lifetime goals. Often this is because we worry more about what others think than about our own personal satisfaction.

If others criticize or speak negatively about your goals and your positive outlook on life, it is often because they do not have the passion or motivation to make changes for themselves.

Be cautious of listening to negative input from others. If they cannot see your aspirations as inspirational then try to spend more time with people who do.

> One of the lessons that I grew up with was to always stay true to yourself and never let what somebody else says distract you from your goals. And so when I hear about negative and false attacks, I really don't invest any energy in them, because I know who I am.
>
> Michelle Obama

My ideas and inspirations

_____

_____

_____

_____

6.12 Face your fears

Fear is a natural, instinctive protection, but it doesn't have to rule our lives. Whether physical or mental, fear generally requires some sort of action. This action will create a momentum that can allow you to overcome the apprehension you are experiencing.

Don't allow your mind to get trapped in the imagination of fear – this isn't real and is often very different to the actual situation you encounter.

Accept fear as a part of life. Write down the things you are afraid of and look at the worst possible outcome. Often there isn't so much to fear after all.

> When you face your fear, most of the time you will discover that it was not really such a big threat after all. We all need some form of deeply rooted, powerful motivation - it empowers us to overcome obstacles so we can live our dreams.
>
> Les Brown

My ideas and inspirations

_____

_____

_____

_____

6.13 If at first you don't succeed...

You've no doubt heard the old adage, "If at first you don't succeed, try, try and try again." This is the attitude you must develop to achieve your greatest goals.

The path to eventual success will be littered with challenges. The opposite of success is not failure – it is giving up.

Don't give up on your goals at the first sign of trouble.

> What we decide to do in the face of adversity is perhaps the truest measure of character.
>
> Ian Usher

My ideas and inspirations

_____

_____

_____

_____

6.14 Be prepared to fail

Failure is simply a necessary stepping stone on the path to success.

Most, if not all, really successful entrepreneurs have experienced multiple failures. You too will most likely encounter failure if you set big goals for yourself.

Start to view failure as a learning experience. If you fear failure consistently, you will never put yourself in situations where failure is possible.

Learn from your failures - there is always something to learn. Know that admission of your failure shows great strength of character. Accept failure as an inevitable part of the journey and take the next step forward confidently.

> Success is the ability to go from one failure to another with no loss of enthusiasm.
>
> Winston Churchill

My ideas and inspirations

_____

_____

_____

_____

6.15 Learn from your mistakes

You will make mistakes – we all do. You are very unlikely to achieve anything of significance in this life without making some mistakes along the way.

Making mistakes is acceptable, but failing to learn from them is not. Each mistake is an opportunity to learn a lesson, a chance to avoid making the same error again. Mistakes aren't bad things. Think of them merely as experiences you need to have in order to find the correct course on route to your ultimate destination.

Some of the most important lessons of life are learnt as a result of bad decisions we make. Good judgment only develops if you truly learn from your mistakes. Don't beat yourself up – learn quickly and move on.

> I've never had a failure in my life – only an educational experience that didn't go my way.
>
> Joe Theismann

My ideas and inspirations

_____

_____

_____

_____

6.16 Don't give up when you are almost there

So many people get very close to what they want to achieve, but fall at the final hurdle.

Your goal can often seem further away, the closer you get to it. Don't make the mistake of giving up when what you want is almost within your reach. Keep the end result in sharp focus and push on to completion.

Don't see completion as the end of a journey. See it as the gateway to the next goal and the forward progression of your life experiences.

> Many of life's failures are people who did not realize how close they were to success when they gave up.
>
> Thomas Alva Edison

My ideas and inspirations

_____

_____

_____

_____

_____

STEP 7

REWARD YOURSELF

When you complete your goal it is important to reward yourself for this achievement.

Look back over your accomplishments and enjoy the satisfaction that success brings.

This will train the subconscious mind to focus on activities that produce successful results.

7.1 Reward yourself for success

The first thing you must do when you achieve a goal is to reward yourself.

Many people find it useful to set rewards in advance. They are an appealing incentive, drawing you onward toward success.

Your reward should be appropriate to the goal you have achieved. A big effort resulting in a big success deserves a suitably big reward.

A reward will train your mind positively and set you up for future victory.

> For every disciplined effort there is a multiple reward.
> Jim Rohn

My ideas and inspirations

_____

_____

_____

_____

_____

7.2 Be proud of your achievements

You are justified in being proud of what you have achieved.

Setting a goal and then working diligently toward it, maintaining focus through any challenges, and ultimately achieving what you set out to do - these things set you apart from others who lack your drive and determination.

Be proud of your successess and enjoy with satisfaction the fruits of your labors.

> Great champions have an enormous sense of pride. The people who excel are those who are driven to show the world and prove to themselves just how good they are.
> Nancy Lopez

My ideas and inspirations

_____

_____

_____

_____

_____

7.3 Set another goal

Once you have enjoyed your success it is time to move forward. Don't lose the motivation you have created.

Set yourself another goal, or pick the next one you wish to tackle from your list.

And this time you can aim even higher, building on your previous accomplishments.

> The achievement of one goal should be the starting point of another.
>
> Alexander Graham Bell

My ideas and inspirations

_____

_____

_____

_____

_____

7.4 It is not luck!!

As you begin to achieve your goals, and enjoy the rewards of doing so, you may start to hear others tell you just how "lucky" you have been in your success.

It may feel easy to smile and agree. However, please recognize that what you have achieved is as a result of something you have created. And luck has had very little to do with it at all.

Perhaps if others worked as hard as you have at achieving their own goals, they might be just as "lucky' as you!

> Luck is what happens when preparation meets opportunity.
> Seneca

My ideas and inspirations

_____

_____

_____

_____

_____

FURTHER INSPIRATION

More tips and ideas to assist you on your journey to goal achieving success.

8.1 Ask yourself what excites you

In his book "The Four Hour Work Week" Tim Ferriss asks a seemingly simple question: "What is the opposite of happiness?" He argues that the answer isn't sadness, as many people would suggest – the opposite of happiness is boredom.

It follows, he suggests, that to live a happy life you simply need to find the things that don't bore you. Discover what excites you and you have the key to your happiness.

Make whatever excites you part of your next goal and you will happily work toward it with enthusiasm.

> I feel sorry for the person who can't get genuinely excited about his work. Not only will he never be satisfied, but he will never achieve anything worthwhile.
>
> Walter Chrysler

My ideas and inspirations

_____

_____

_____

_____

_____

8.2 Save money to fund your goals

Many goals will require some sort of financial input. Part of achieving such a goal is to come up with the necessary funds.

It can be helpful to set up a separate account and add funds to it regularly. Perhaps each time you receive some income you could set aside a percentage, adding it to your "goal achievement account".

If you consciously "save" money when buying something new, add the "saved" amount to your goal fund.

> Money doesn't change men, it merely unmasks them. If a man is naturally selfish or arrogant or greedy, the money brings that out, that's all.
>
> Henry Ford

My ideas and inspirations

_____

_____

_____

_____

_____

8.3 Learn to listen

It is often said that we have two ears and one mouth, and we should use them in that proportion.

It is very difficult to learn anything, or to find out new information, while talking. Practice the habit of listening attentively to what others have to say.

What you learn may be something that helps you toward your goal.

> Learn to listen, then listen to learn.
>
> Ian Usher

My ideas and inspirations

_____

_____

_____

_____

_____

8.4 Help others to achieve their goals

By listening to others you can discover what they are trying to achieve. Perhaps you can assist them to move toward their goals a well as your own.

This will serve to increase your own motivation too. The more you help others, the more you will attract others to help you.

> You can have everything in life you want, if you will just help other people get what they want.
>
> Zig Ziglar

My ideas and inspirations

_____

_____

_____

_____

8.5 Develop a "mission statement"

The term "mission statement" is a phrase used by many businesses, big and small. It distils the company ethos and its guiding beliefs down to one or two succinct sentences. It captures the very essence of the company, their reason for being.

If it is important enough for a company to have a mission statement, then surely your life merits one too. Your mission statement outlines what it is you feel your life is supposed to be about – what it is you should be doing with your life.

Your mission statement will assist with goal achievement if both are aligned.

> Just as your car runs more smoothly and requires less energy to go faster and farther when the wheels are in perfect alignment, you perform better when your thoughts, feelings, emotions, goals, and values are in balance.
>
> Brian Tracy

My ideas and inspirations

_____

_____

_____

_____

8.6 Copy genius

If you want to be successful, the simplest way is to model success. Find someone who is an expert at what you are trying to achieve and simply mirror what they do.

If their actions have resulted in the same sort of achievement you are aiming for, then doing the same thing increases your chances of success immensely.

You'll probably find out that all they are doing is working hard and working consistently. Do the same with passion and enthusiasm and you will no doubt move effortlessly toward your chosen objectives.

> *Genius is one percent inspiration and ninety-nine percent perspiration.*
>
> Thomas Alva Edison

My ideas and inspirations

_____

_____

_____

_____

_____

8.7 Do the right thing

In your heart you will know what you should be doing to move toward the ultimate achievement of your goal. Don't get distracted by other less important, irrelevant matters.

When faced with a choice of what to do, ask yourself one simple question: "What is the right thing to do now?"

This is good advice for every choice you face in life. If you constantly ask yourself this question, and listen to your own answers you will be amazed by the changes that occur.

> Keep true, never be ashamed of doing right; decide on what you think is right and stick to it.
>
> T.S. Eliot

My ideas and inspirations

_____

_____

_____

_____

_____

8.8 Think and act differently

To achieve your goals you may have to change many of your actions and habits.

If you want to stay the same, carry on doing what you have always done. If you want to change your eventual outcomes, you are going to have to start to think and act differently.

Think outside of your comfort zone and with originality. You will stand apart from your peers.

> *You are the embodiment of the information you choose to accept and act upon. To change your circumstances you need to change your thinking and subsequent actions.*
> Adlin Sinclair

My ideas and inspirations

_____

_____

_____

_____

_____

8.9 Expand your comfort zone

Life is supposed to be an adventure, filled with challenges, excitement and thrills. It is not meant to be lived swaddled in a blanket of safety and fear.

When you begin to tackle your goals you are going to have to step out of your comfort zone as you take on new challenges.

It is only when in this new territory, where you are uncomfortable, that true personal growth occurs.

> True greatness or achievement only happens when you push yourself beyond your comfort zone.
>
> Ian Usher

My ideas and inspirations

_____

_____

_____

_____

_____

8.10 Don't be put off by negativity

By thinking and acting differently, by beginning to achieve new things, and by pushing beyond your comfort zone, you may find that you will challenge others in your peer group.

For those unwilling or unable to make a commitment to improve their own destiny, it is sometimes easier to criticize those who are moving onward. This is almost inevitable.

Refuse to listen to or be affected by negativity. Be aware that this negativity is only a reflection of the thoughts of the negative person, not of your actions or choices.

> Dogs don't bark at parked cars
>
> Anonymous

My ideas and inspirations

_____

_____

_____

_____

8.11 Continue to choose your words carefully

Always remember that how you speak is both a reflection on your inner thoughts and an influence on your subsequent actions. Continue to be careful about what you think and say.

If you say you "can't" do something, then you almost certainly won't be able to do it. If you say "I'll try" you may as well add the phrase "but I'll probably fail too".

If you talk about your "dreams" and "desires", you most likely won't achieve as much as if you simply change the word to "goals". A dream is merely a goal without a timeline.

> A goal is not the same as a desire, and this is an important distinction to make. You can have a desire you don't intend to act on. But you can't have a goal you don't intend to act on.
>
> Tom Morris

My ideas and inspirations

_____

_____

_____

_____

8.12 Think "out of the box"

Creative thinking can produce innovative solutions to current challenges. Learn to be open to unusual ideas and solutions.

Examine challenges from all sides, think of different ways to overcome obstacles, and don't immediately discard ideas that seem odd or unusual.

Practice spontaneity.

The more you can act without too much thought, the more you will be able to overcome fears and anxieties. Then your mind will be clear to focus on the important aspects of your goals.

> Innovation distinguishes between a leader and a follower.
> Steve Jobs

My ideas and inspirations

_____

_____

_____

_____

_____

8.13 Believe in yourself

Belief in your own abilities is a key factor for goal achievement. You have to be able to see yourself achieving the task you have set.

Don't allow self-doubt to creep in unnoticed.

Constant positive reinforcement will keep you focused on your target and assured of success.

> It is easy to have faith in yourself and have discipline when you are a winner, when you are number one. What you have got to have is faith and discipline when you are not yet a winner.
>
> Vince Lombardi

My ideas and inspirations

_____

_____

_____

_____

_____

8.14 Control your responses to affect outcomes

When working toward your goals, events beyond your control will inevitably reveal challenges you didn't foresee.

Although you may have no control over these events, you can control how you react to them. Don't treat every challenge as negative. Try to identify a positive outcome or learn something that will help you move forward, and then respond accordingly. What many see as adversity, others simply call adventure.

It is all about your own perception. Often challenges provide opportunities that would have otherwise been overlooked.

> Stop the mindless wishing that things would be different. Rather than wasting time and emotional and spiritual energy in explaining why we don't have what we want, we can start to pursue other ways to get it.
>
> Greg Anderson

My ideas and inspirations

_____

_____

_____

_____

8.15 Strive for continual improvement

Keep moving forward, trying to improve on what you have previously achieved. You can't achieve your goals without progressing forward.

Once you have completed a goal you need to set yourself another. Stretch yourself by setting your sights higher for your next challenge. Reflect on what you have learnt and take this forward.

It is easy to live life within the narrow confines of your comfort zone, but in this small safe haven there is little opportunity for excitement, success or achievement. Test yourself as often as you can.

Challenge yourself to attain new heights, take on bigger tasks and strive for greater results.

> Progress always involves risk; you can't steal second base and keep your foot on first base.
>
> Frederick Wilcox

My ideas and inspirations

_____

_____

_____

_____

8.16 Learn to spot opportunities

Opportunities abound – you just have to become good at spotting them and acting quickly and spontaneously to take advantage of any occasion. Become an expert at spotting all possibilities.

Opportunities can often present themselves as challenges, but by overcoming challenges you can propel yourself toward your target quickly and successfully.

Always keep an open mind. Question everything and look at opportunities and challenges from all viewpoints.

> Opportunities are like buses, there is always another one coming.
>
> Richard Branson

My ideas and inspirations

_____

_____

_____

_____

_____

8.17 Make your work support your lifestyle

Don't spend forty or more years of your life trapped in a job you don't like or enjoy. Discover your passion and then formulate a plan to use that passion to generate or contribute to your income.

Life is far too short to waste it away doing things you don't want to do. Get creative and figure out how you and your family can live the lives you really want to.

Look at all of your options, and remember that children can be home-schooled and often benefit greatly from living alternatively and outside of the strict and often limiting educational system.

> Make your vocation into vacation and you will not have to work a single day.
>
> Nicholas Lore

My ideas and inspirations

_____

_____

_____

_____

_____

8.18 Take responsibility

Your own success, and ultimately your own life, is your responsibility. Nobody else is going to do any of this for you. Whilst others may guide, help or contribute along the way, it is ultimately up to you, and you alone, to set your goals and create your success.

You can choose to allow life to push you around, hoping that it will all be better one day, or you can decide to take responsibility for your own life and future success.

Write down your goals, get to work on them and create your own life – the life that you really want to live. Don't compromise your future by failing to act in the present.

> Each player must accept the cards life deals him or her: but once they are in hand, he or she alone must decide how to play the cards in order to win the game.
>
> Voltaire

My ideas and inspirations

_____

_____

_____

_____

8.19 Trust your instincts

Malcolm Gladwell's book "Blink" discusses moments when we experience an instinctive feeling, almost immediately after we meet someone or encounter a new idea.

Our first impression is usually correct and that assessment is based upon thousands of tiny pieces of information that our subconscious mind collects and processes in the "blink" of an eye.

As a secondary process, your mind presents plenty of reasons to doubt this initial assessment, which distorts that original "blink moment". Trust your instincts. Go with your gut feeling, because more often than not, that decision will be the correct one for you.

> If the single man plant himself indomitably on his instincts, and there abide, the huge world will come round to him.
> Ralph Waldo Emerson

My ideas and inspirations

_____

_____

_____

_____

8.20 Do the opposite

It is said that only one or two percent of the population write down their goals. A similar proportion of the population actually achieves any level of success or happiness with which they are content.

It is no coincidence that there is a significant correlation between these two groups.

Don't be like everyone else in the way you think and act. Look at what most people do and do the opposite. Steer for yourself a very different course through life, based on your own goals and aspirations.

> The ninety and nine are with dreams, content, but the hope of the world made new, is the hundredth man who is grimly bent on making those dreams come true.
>
> Edgar Allan Poe

My ideas and inspirations

_____

_____

_____

_____

8.21 Learn to say "No" to time wasting

One of the biggest steps you can make toward the achievement of your goals is learning to say "No".

Say an emphatic "No" to time-wasting activities. Do you want to waste your time hypnotized by meaningless soap operas on TV each evening? Wouldn't a better use of this time be to take some action that propels you toward your goals?

You may also have to say "No" to time wasting people. You know the people in your life who sap your time and energy and who offer no support in your journey toward success.

Time is precious and time wasted can never be regained. Ensure you invest your time wisely.

> You may delay, but time will not, and lost time is never found again.
>
> Benjamin Franklin

My ideas and inspirations

_____

_____

_____

_____

8.22 Don't justify yourself or your goals

Your goals are exactly that – yours!! You do not need to justify your plans or your goals to anyone else. Some people have no concept of why someone else would, for example, want to go skydiving!

Don't feel you have to justify your goals to anyone who doesn't understand them, or perhaps doesn't agree with them. If you do it will undermine your confidence and hamper your progress.

Each person's goals are unique and individual - they require no explanation.

> Be who you are and say what you feel, because those who mind don't matter and those who matter don't mind.
>
> Dr. Seuss

My ideas and inspirations

_____

_____

_____

_____

_____

8.23 Do what you want, not what others expect

Our peer group, and society in general, place certain expectations on us. It is our choice, however, whether we conform to these expectations or not.

Do you wish to live your life as someone else would have you live it, or are you going to decide how to live it for yourself?

It is sometimes hard to stand alone, but when you achieve something from this place, you will experience a feeling of elation that really does make it all worthwhile.

> True happiness is to enjoy the present, without anxious dependence upon the future.
>
> Seneca

My ideas and inspirations

_____

_____

_____

_____

_____

8.24 See the bigger picture

It is all too easy to get bogged down in the detail of the day-to-day tasks you need to complete as you journey toward your ultimate goal.

Sometimes you just have to take things one step at a time, concentrating on the task at hand. However, this can be made easier when you maintain an overall view of what you eventually plan to achieve.

When you have to deal with multiple goal lists you may become overwhelmed. Don't forget to look at where you have come from and where you are heading – keep the bigger picture in mind at all times.

> The journey of a thousand miles begins with one step.
> Lao Tzu

My ideas and inspirations

_____

_____

_____

_____

8.25 Feed your passion

We have mentioned building excitement around your goals and having a powerful motivating reason for the items on your list. You need to work continuously on feeding this passion.

Read about others' achievements. Watch videos or movies. Put pictures up in prominent places. Go to meetings, events and seminars. Re-read this book.

Feed your passion at every opportunity and your mind will automatically get to work on creating the outcomes that you desire.

> To be successful you've got to have a dream, a vision, a burning passion, a magnificent obsession. This dream, goal, obsession has to become your prime motivator. It takes enthusiasm, commitment, pride, a willingness to work hard, a willingness to go the extra mile, a willingness to do whatever has to be done in order to get the job done.
> Jeffrey J. Mayer

My ideas and inspirations

_____

_____

_____

_____

8.26 Learn from your past

We have talked about learning from your mistakes and accepting failure as just another step toward eventual success. However, your past can also provide you with other insightful information.

When were you happiest? What have you always enjoyed doing? What do you dislike? What do you really hate doing? What did you find most challenging?

Look into your past to find answers relevant to your present. Your past gives you a sense of who you are and what you want. Learn to be true to yourself. Make sure your goals are aligned with who you are and step confidently into your future.

> By three methods we may learn wisdom: First, by reflection, which is noblest; second, by imitation, which is easiest; and third by experience, which is the bitterest.
>
> Confucius

My ideas and inspirations

_____

_____

_____

_____

8.27 Visualize your future

We have also mentioned using visualization as a method to catapult you toward the success you are targeting.

The more vividly you can imagine your future, the more quickly you will progress to your ultimate achievement. Don't just imagine it - write it down.

> How would you feel if you had mastered and attained all your goals a year from now? How would you feel about yourself? How would you feel about your life? Answering these questions will help you develop compelling reasons to achieve your goals. Having a powerful enough "why" will provide you with the necessary "how". Take this opportunity to brainstorm your top four one-year goals. Under each one, write a paragraph about why you are absolutely committed to achieving these goals within the year.
>
> Anthony Robbins

My ideas and inspirations

_____

_____

_____

_____

8.28 Act now, in the present

Once you have examined your past and decided upon how you want your future to be, the next step is simple – just do it – take action.

Take just one step, the first step necessary to start you on your way. It sounds pretty obvious, but this first step is often the hardest of all the steps you will take on route to your goal.

This first step is usually the one that takes you outside of your comfort zone. But once taken, the second step will be easier and all subsequent steps even more so.

> Learn from the past, set vivid, detailed goals for the future, and live in the only moment of time over which you have any control - now.
>
> Denis Waitley

My ideas and inspirations

_____

_____

_____

_____

_____

8.29 Invest in yourself

See all time and money spent as an investment.

Books, audio materials, training courses and seminars are not expenses, they are investments.

Time spent reading, listening, learning and planning is not a waste, it is an investment.

Don't short-change yourself.

Any investment in yourself is an investment in your future success.

> What you get by achieving your goals is not as important as what you become by achieving your goals.
> Henry David Thoreau

My ideas and inspirations

_____

_____

_____

_____

_____

8.30 Don't worry

If you have issues that are causing you concern, there are usually only two possible scenarios. Either you are able to do something about the matter that is troubling you, or it is something that is completely out of your control and nothing you can do will make things any different.

If it is the former, then stop worrying, and do something about it. Action will dispel the worry.

If there is nothing you can do about it, all the worrying in the world won't change a thing. Learn what you can, let go of the worry and quickly move on.

> Be careful what you water your dreams with. Water them with worry and fear and you will produce weeds that choke the life from your dream. Water them with optimism and solutions and you will cultivate success.
>
> Lao Tzu

My ideas and inspirations

_____

_____

_____

_____

8.31 Whatever you do in life, give 100%

Life is supposed to be an adventure.

When you decide how you want your adventure to unfold, give it all you have got. Live large and enjoy the journey.

One day soon you'll be very glad you did.

> Life is an adventure. We all only get one go at this. My firm belief is that we should try to live life's adventure to the best of our ability.
>
> Ian Usher

My ideas and inspirations

_____

_____

_____

_____

CONCLUSION

A NOTE FROM IAN USHER:

> If you want to live a happy life, tie it to a goal, not to people or things.
>
> Albert Einstein

The life I have lived for the past few decades has been a testament to the power of setting goals and working diligently toward them. Goals have shaped the life I have created to this point, and they continue to be important for the future I plan to work toward.

However, in the writing of this book it has become very obvious that happiness is intrinsically linked to setting, working toward and achieving goals. In a talk I did for a TEDx event in Vienna in 2013, I suggested that the audience should ask themselves two very important questions. Both of those questions are referenced in this book.

The subject for the day of talks in Vienna was "Unlimited", and I was specifically asked to speak on the topic of living an unlimited lifestyle. I found that to discuss living without some of the limits others perceive required me to talk not only about lifestyle, but also about goals and the very nature of happiness.

You can view the TEDxVienna talk here:

www.IanUsher.com/speaker.php

Whilst these subjects are all fundamentally linked, the real foundation for creating happiness and an improved lifestyle is to work toward a set of well planned, challenging and rewarding goals.

Start by writing them down and then have the courage to take that first step.

I promise you will be amazed by the results.

Good luck with all of your goals.

> Goals are a means to an end, not the ultimate purpose of our lives. They are simply a tool to concentrate our focus and move us in a direction. The only reason we really pursue goals is to cause ourselves to expand and grow. Achieving goals by themselves will never make us happy in the long term; it's who you become, as you overcome the obstacles necessary to achieve your goals, that can give you the deepest and most long-lasting sense of fulfillment.
>
> Anthony Robbins

A NOTE FROM VANESSA ANDERSON:

 I can accept anything, except what seems to be the easiest for most people: the half-way, the almost, the just-about, the in-between.

Ayn Rand

Since I was a child, I have stood alone and questioned the world and people around me. I guess I never wanted to be one of the "masses". My life has been challenging and difficult at times, but also immensely fulfilling. I have experienced personal growth on an ongoing basis and there hasn't been a single moment of regret.

Every year I set myself at least five new goals. Sometimes these were undemanding tasks, just something I'd never tried or experienced. But every year these goals drove me toward bigger, more taxing life experiences.

I stepped out of my comfort zone whenever I could. If I became aware of something that I was fearful of, I would organize an activity to overcome that fear. I learned early on to embrace change, so much so that I now welcome change whenever I feel that life has become unchallenging, "stuck" or unfulfilling in anyway.

It isn't always easy. Living life in this way sometimes alienates friends and family. There can be a lack of security which is a mindset that has to be overcome.

But as I've grown older I've transformed this issue of security into seeing that life is short and so needs to be lived in the moment more and more.

I met Ian in a random moment early in 2013 having just made some radical changes in my life. We spent just one evening chatting in London, but I knew I had met someone who was aligned to my way of thinking and living.

Within just a few months, I had moved to Central America. I gave up my job in London, sold my house and relocated to live with someone I barely knew. This I did pretty much overnight – I trusted the "blink" moment and stepped once again into a new and challenging situation.

I believe I live my life honestly and without compromise, facing each new adventure head on. I have not remained long in any environment that has left me uninspired.

I hope this book and my short story inspires you to live life in the way that you want to – don't give up on your goals and aspirations. They are what make life truly fulfilling and enjoyable.

> Our dreams and goals are never completely realized. They are always there before our eyes, but always just slightly out of reach. And so, as we strive to fulfill our vision, we must make the most of every living moment.
>
> Jacqueline Onassis

ABOUT THE AUTHORS

In 2008 Ian listed his "entire life" for sale on eBay in order to work on his list of lifetime goals. He traveled the globe for two years, working on a list of 100 goals, bound by a challenging timeline of 100 weeks.

He wrote his first book, "A Life Sold", about this amazing journey, and Walt Disney Pictures bought the movie rights to his incredible story. With Walt Disney's check in hand, Ian decided the next part of life's adventure would involve buying a private Caribbean island. He chronicles his adventures in this challenging location in his second book, "Paradise Delayed".

Ian now speaks for organizations around the world, helping others to set and achieve their own goals.

Vanessa too is a traveler and adventurer and has lived in several different countries in Europe. This book is her first foray into the world of publishing.

Ian and Vanessa's paths crossed in London in 2013, and their adventurous lives have become intertwined since then.

They have a long list of goals.

More info at:

www.IanUsher.com

www.DivergingRoads.com

SUGGESTED FURTHER READING

Here are a just a few timeless classics that will help you on your goal achieving journey:

- The 7 Habits of Highly Effective People by Stephen Covey
- How To Win Friends and Influence People by Dale Carnegie
- Think & Grow Rich by Napoleon Hill
- As a Man Thinketh by James Allen
- Live Your Dreams by Les Brown
- Losing My Virginity by Richard Branson
- The 4 Hour Work Week by Tim Ferriss
- Multiple Streams of Income by Robert G Allen
- 7 Strategies for Wealth & Happiness by Jim Rohn
- Chicken Soup for the Soul by Jack Canfield and Mark Victor Hansen
- Awaken the Giant Within by Anthony Robbins

Go to:

www.IanUsher.com/goals

for further suggestions and links to even more inspirational ideas.

APPENDIX
100 GOAL ACHIEVING TIPS

STEP 1: WRITE IT DOWN
1.1 Write down your goal
1.2 Make a list
1.3 Get SMART about your goal
1.4 Write down your goal every day

STEP 2: SET A DEADLINE
2.1 Make a plan
2.2 Set a deadline
2.3 Start with an easy goal
2.4 Break down a large goal into smaller steps
2.5 Set up a website
2.6 Use a diary for planning

STEP 3: WORK ON YOUR MINDSET
3.1 Adjust your attitude
3.2 Get inspired by your goals
3.3 Set your sights on the end result
3.4 Use visualization
3.5 Dream big
3.6 Make your goals realistic
3.7 Keep an open mind
3.8 Develop a positive outlook
3.9 Listen to audios
3.10 Read positive books
3.11 Attend a seminar
3.12 Listen to powerful, uplifting music
3.13 Watch an inspirational movie
3.14 Your goal has already been achieved!
3.15 Spend time with other goal-oriented people
3.16 Develop a hunger for your goal
3.17 Increase your energy levels
3.18 Embrace change
3.19 Expect to succeed
3.20 Act as if your goal is already achieved

STEP 4: DEVELOP YOUR SKILLSET
4.1	Research your goals
4.2	Develop your skillset
4.3	Read an instructional book
4.4	Book a course
4.5	Apply focus
4.6	Ask for help
4.7	Find a mentor

STEP 5: TAKE THE FIRST STEP
5.1	Take the first step
5.2	Do the important things first
5.3	Be accountable to someone else
5.4	Use your time productively
5.5	Use visual reminders
5.6	Computer desktop background
5.7	Screensaver images
5.8	Make a vision board
5.9	Document your progress
5.10	Apply positive internal dialogue
5.11	Do it even when you don't want to
5.12	Do what you need to do, not what you want to do

STEP 6: CONTINUE TO COMPLETION
6.1	Make a commitment to yourself
6.2	Take action every day
6.3	Reaffirm your goal every day
6.4	Enjoy the journey
6.5	Flexibility is the key
6.6	Identify your negative traits
6.7	Don't go back to your old ways
6.8	Don't run from problems
6.9	Shed your excuses
6.10	Be prepared to make sacrifices
6.11	Don't worry about what others think
6.12	Face your fears
6.13	If at first you don't succeed…
6.14	Be prepared to fail
6.15	Learn from your mistakes
6.16	Don't give up when you are almost there

STEP 7: REWARD YOURSELF

7.1	Reward yourself for success
7.2	Be proud of your achievements
7.3	Set another goal
7.4	It is not luck!!

SOME FURTHER INSPIRATION

8.1	Ask yourself what excites you
8.2	Save money to fund your goals
8.3	Learn to listen
8.4	Help others to achieve their goals
8.5	Develop a "mission statement"
8.6	Copy genius
8.7	Do the right thing
8.8	Think and act differently
8.9	Expand your comfort zone
8.10	Don't be put off by negativity
8.11	Continue to choose your words carefully
8.12	Think "out of the box"
8.13	Believe in yourself
8.14	Control your responses to affect outcomes
8.15	Strive for continual improvement
8.16	Learn to spot opportunities
8.17	Make your work support your lifestyle
8.18	Take responsibility
8.19	Trust your instincts
8.20	Do the opposite
8.21	Learn to say "No" to time wasting
8.22	Don't justify yourself or your goals
8.23	Do what you want, not what others expect
8.24	See the bigger picture
8.25	Feed your passion
8.26	Learn from your past
8.27	Visualize your future
8.28	Act now, in the present
8.29	Invest in yourself
8.30	Don't worry
8.31	Whatever you do in life, give 100%

ALSO BY THE SAME AUTHOR
www.IanUsher.com/writer.php

A Life Sold

What on earth would make someone decide to put their whole life up for sale... on eBay?

When Ian Usher decided that it was time to leave the past behind and move on to the next chapter of his life, that is exactly what he did. The results were surprising, entertaining and challenging.

However, the auction was only the beginning of the adventure. What does someone do when they have sold their life? Well, just about anything they like really!

Armed with a list of 100 lifetime goals, and a self-imposed timeframe of 100 weeks, Ian embarked on what could truly be described as the journey of a lifetime – a global adventure spanning six continents, two years, and almost every emotion.

From the amazing highs of achievement, happiness and love, to the terrible lows of disappointment, loneliness and despair, come along and enjoy the rollercoaster ride of life, as experienced by one traveller who is simply looking for a new start.

Paradise Delayed

What does someone do after putting their whole life up for sale on eBay, then travelling the world for two years with a list of 100 lifetime goals and a challenging timeframe of 100 weeks, and finally selling the rights for the whole amazing story to Walt Disney Pictures?

Why, they go and buy their own private Caribbean island, of course!

The author's continuing quest for amazing adventures and incredible experiences take him to the beautiful tropical archipelago of Bocas del Toro, on the Caribbean coast of Panama. There he somehow ends up purchasing his own private Caribbean island - it sounds like a dream come true, doesn't it?

Maybe not! The trials and tribulations of a gringo trying to make a home on an overgrown island make for a fascinating portrayal of life in this challenging area of the world.

Sinking boats, defective chainsaws, document forgery and aggressive roosters are just a small sample of the hurdles facing a tired traveller who really just wants to lie in a hammock sipping margaritas for a while!

"Paradise Delayed" may make you re-consider the nature of the Caribbean island dream, or may just inspire you to find your own adventure of a lifetime.

www.ingramcontent.com/pod-product-compliance
Lightning Source LLC
LaVergne TN
LVHW041546070426
835507LV00011B/946